Contents

Welcome to the hospital!

This is the hospital.

4

5

Working in the hospital

Lots of people work in the hospital.

It is a very busy place.

We drive sick people to hospital in an **ambulance**.

9

The doctor

I am a doctor. I will find out what is wrong with you.

This **stethoscope** will help me listen to your heart.

11

The nurse

I am a nurse.
I will look
after you.

This **thermometer** will help me to take your **temperature**.

In an operation

In an **operation** I wear gloves and a mask.

They stop me from giving you **germs**.

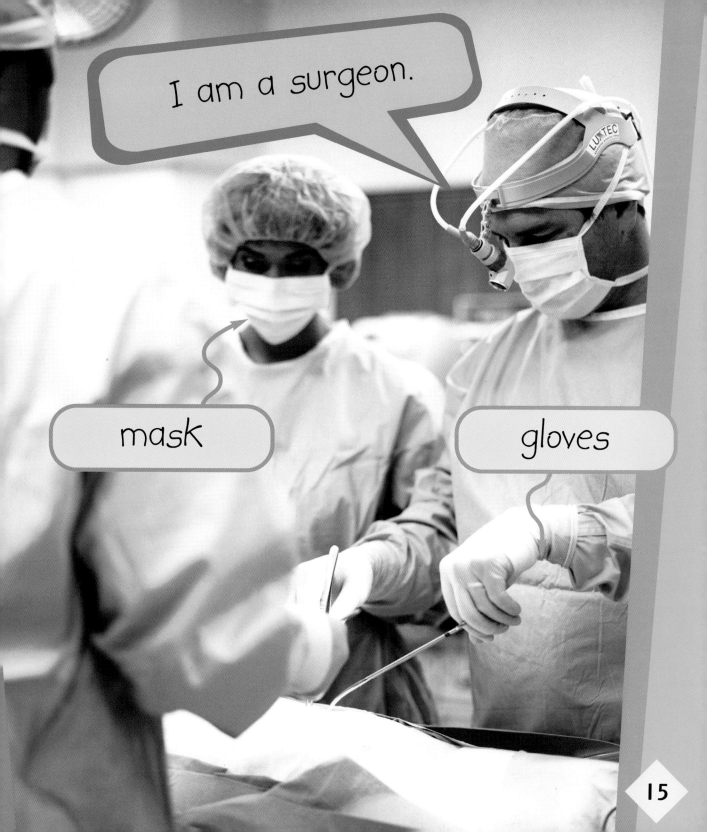

15

Hospital uniforms

doctor

We wear **uniforms** in the hospital.

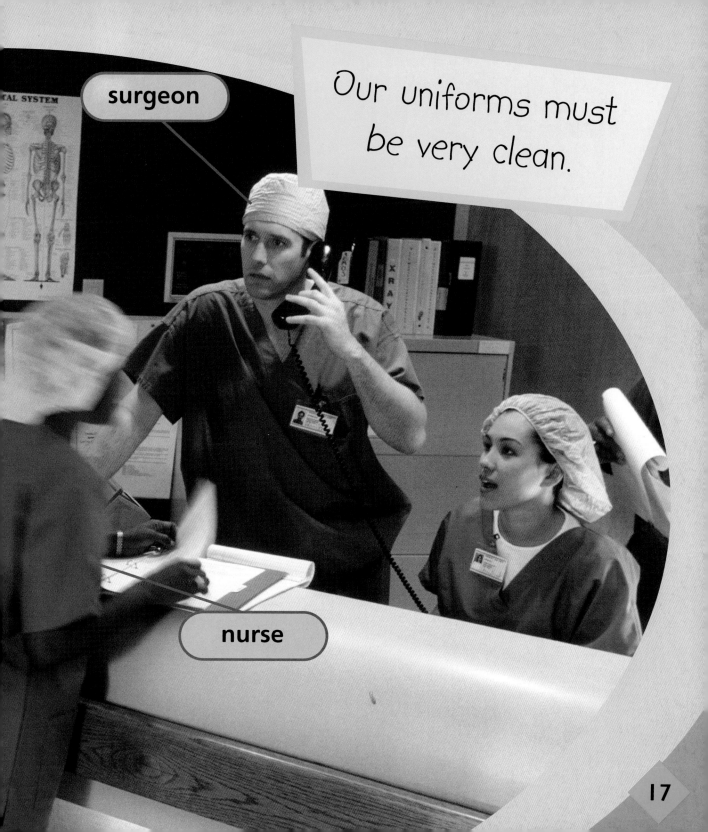

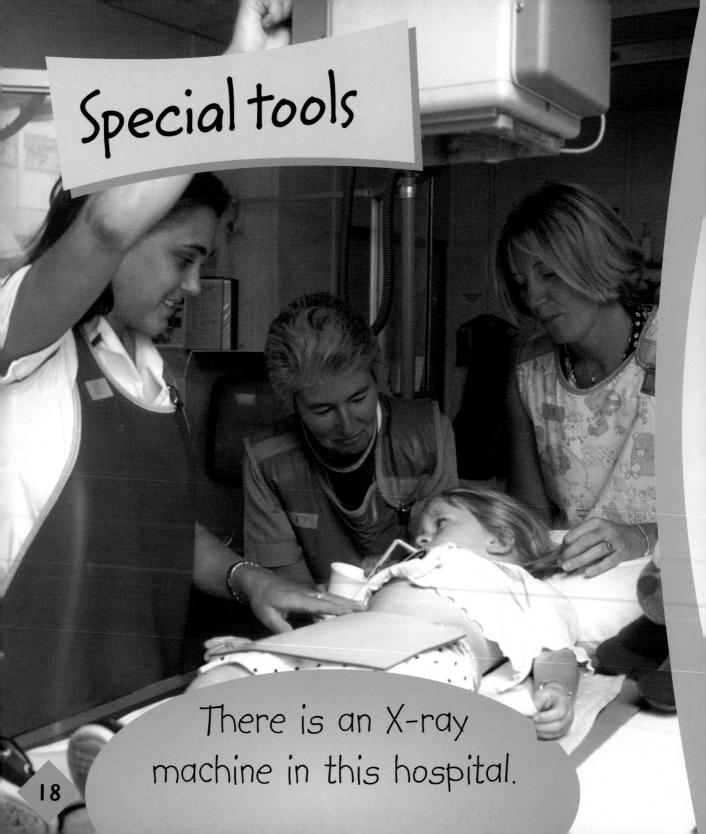

Special tools

There is an X-ray machine in this hospital.

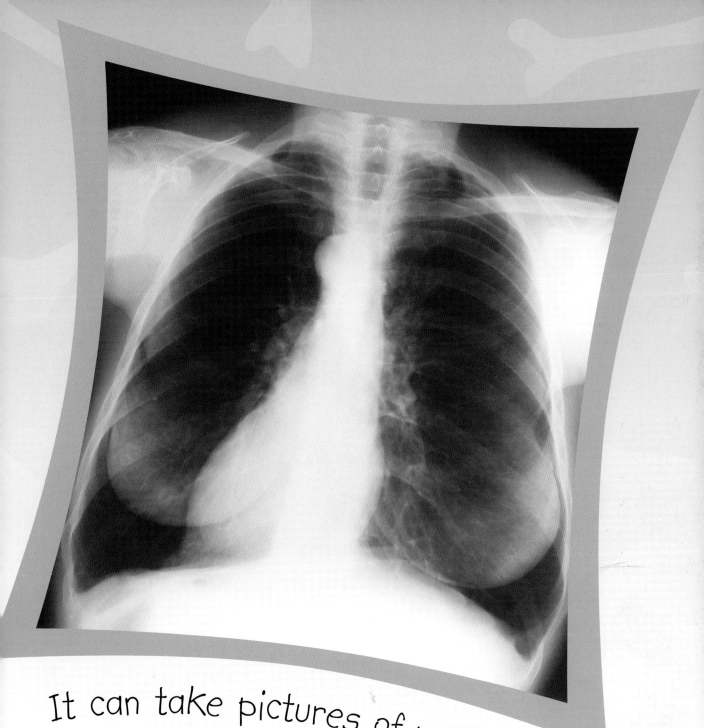

It can take pictures of your bones.

19

Getting better

We mend broken bones by putting them in plaster.

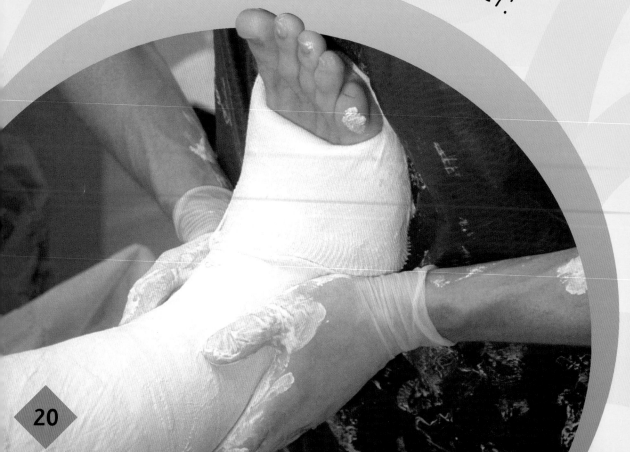

We are always happy when we can make someone better!

21

Quiz

space food

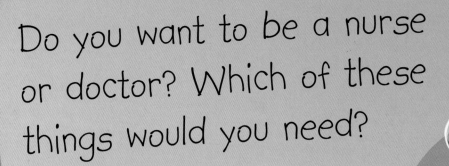

Do you want to be a nurse or doctor? Which of these things would you need?

stethoscope

spacesuit

helmet

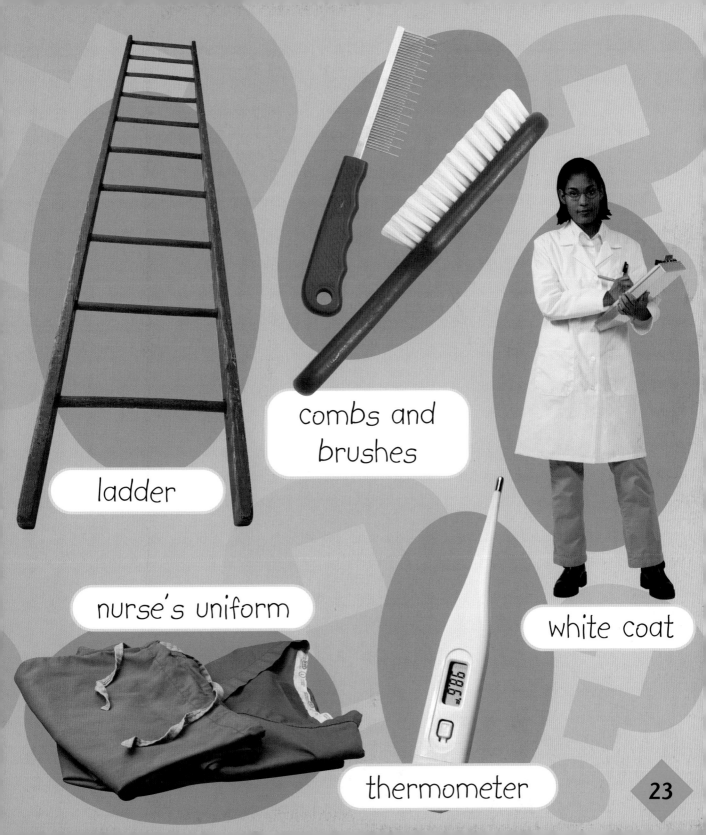

ladder

combs and brushes

nurse's uniform

white coat

thermometer

23

Glossary

ambulance special truck that takes people to hospital

germs things in the air that can make you ill

operation a way of making a person better

stethoscope what a doctor uses to listen to your heart beat

temperature how hot you are

thermometer what a nurse uses to take your temperature

uniform special clothes the doctors and nurses wear at work

Index

Notes for adults

This series supports the young child's exploration of their learning environment and their knowledge and understanding of their world. The following Early Learning Goals are relevant to the series:

• Respond to significant experiences, showing a range of feelings where appropriate.
• Find out about events they observe.
• Ask questions about why things happen and how things work.
• Find out and identify the uses of everyday technology to support their learning.

The series shows the different jobs professionals do in four different environments. There are opportunities to compare and contrast the jobs and provide an understanding of what each entails.

The books will help the child to extend their vocabulary, as they will hear new words. Some of the words that may be new to them in **We Work at the Hospital** are *operation, germs, thermometer, temperature,* and *stethoscope*. Since the words are used in context in the book this should enable the young child to gradually incorporate them into their own vocabulary.

Follow-up activities
The child could role play situations in a hospital. Areas could be set up to create a waiting room, operating theatre, or ambulance. The child could also record what they have found out by drawing, painting, or tape recording their experiences.

24

ital

ore

C153704803

www.heinemann.co.uk/library
Visit our website to find out more information about **Heinemann Library** books.

To order:
☎ Phone 44 (0) 1865 888066
📄 Send a fax to 44 (0) 1865 314091
💻 Visit the Heinemann Bookshop at www.heinemann.co.uk/library to browse our catalogue and order online.

First published in Great Britain by Heinemann Library, Halley Court, Jordan Hill, Oxford OX2 8EJ, part of Harcourt Education.
Heinemann is a registered trademark of Harcourt Education Ltd.

Editorial: Isabel Thomas and Sarah Chappelow
Design: Jo Hinton-Malivoire and bigtop
Picture Research: Erica Newbery
Production: Duncan Gilbert

Originated by RMW
Printed and bound in China by South China Printing Company

ISBN: 978 0 431 16489 2 (hardback)
10 09 08 07
10 9 8 7 6 5 4 3 2 1

ISBN: 978 0 431 16494 6 (paperback)
11 10 09 08 07
10 9 8 7 6 5 4 3 2 1

British Library Cataloguing in Publication Data
Aylmore, Angela
We work at the hospital. - (Where we work)
610.6'9
A full catalogue record for this book is available from the British Library.

Acknowledgements
The publishers would like to thank the following for permission to reproduce photographs:
Alamy pp. **18** (Janine Wiedel Photolibrary), **20** (Medical-on-Line); Corbis p. **21** (Jim Craigmyle); Getty Images pp. **4–5** (Photodisc), **6–7** (Taxi), **10–11** (Taxi/Gary Buss), **11** bottom (Photodisc), **12** (Photodisc/Keith Brofsky), **13** (Photodisc), **15** (Stone/Charles Thatcher); Photos.com pp. **16**, **17**, **19**; Stockbyte Royalty Free Photos pp. **8–9**.

Quiz pp. **22–23**: **astronaut** (Getty/Photodisc), **brush and comb** (Corbis/DK Limited), **doctor** (Getty Images/Photodisc), **firefighter helmet** (Corbis), **ladder** (Corbis/Royalty Free), **scrubs** (Corbis), **space food** (Alamy/Hugh Threlfall), **stethoscope** (Getty Images/Photodisc), **thermometer** (Getty Images/Photodisc).

Cover photograph of a doctor reproduced with permission of Stockbyte Royalty Free Photos.

Every effort has been made to contact copyright holders of any material reproduced in this book. Any omissions will be rectified in subsequent printings if notice is given to the publishers.
The paper used to print this book comes from sustainable resources.

Some words are shown in bold, **like this**. They are explained in the glossary on page 24.